Little Louie Comes Home

{a storybook journal for new and seasoned moms}

By: Nicole R. Montanez

This book is dedicated to all Women. Women who wanted to be moms, were on the fence about being a mom, and those who flat out said no to being a mom. Congratulations you are all MOMS. Let the journey begin!

Little Louie Comes Home

{a storybook journal for new and seasoned moms}

By: Nicole R. Montanez

"WAKE UP!"

-screams Mommy,
as she jumps
out of bed.

Daddy is still sleeping.
He didn't hear a word
she said.

The baby is coming,
today is the day.

Little Louie will be here
hip hip hooray!

Daddy finally jumps up,
not knowing what to do.

Mommy tosses him the phone
and says "call Dr. Sue!"

Once they get to the hospital,
the nurse checks them in.

After they get to the room
the pushing begins.

Mommy closes her eyes and
says a prayer to God.

*"Thank you, Dear God, for the blessing to
come. I love him already, your gift to me,
my precious son."*

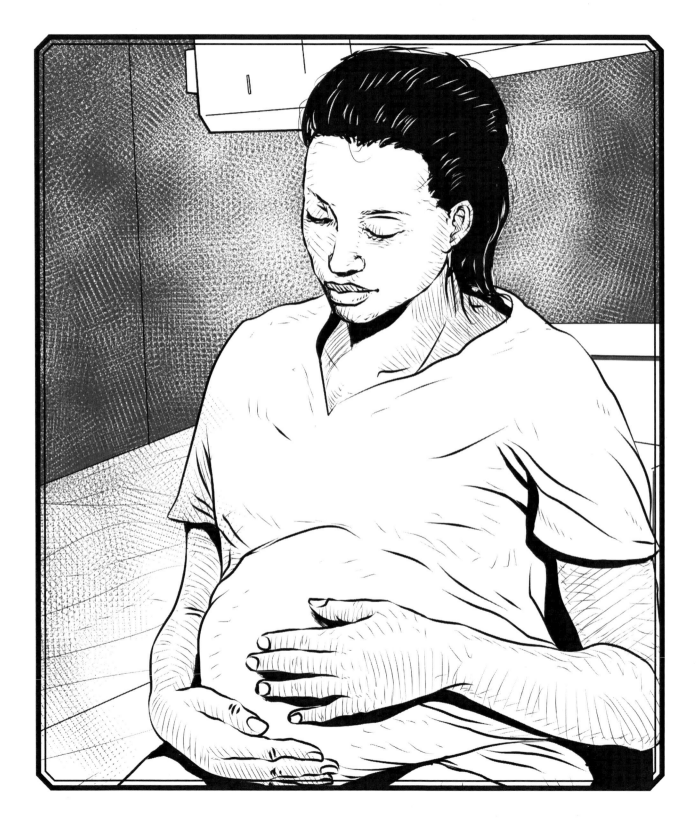

She takes a deep breath and opens her eyes. Before she knows it, she hears a tiny cry.

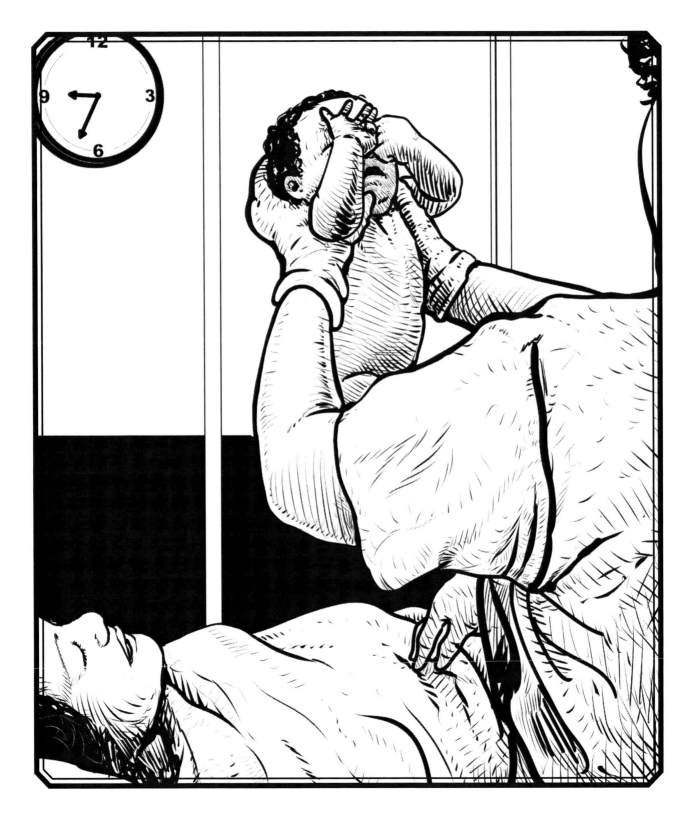

Little Louie is here!
He's perfect and they
are in love.

Daddy can't stop thanking
our Heavenly Father above.

He kisses Mommy's forehead and reaches for the baby.

Little Louie has jet black hair,
almond shaped eyes,
10 fingers ,10 toes
and the cutest button nose.

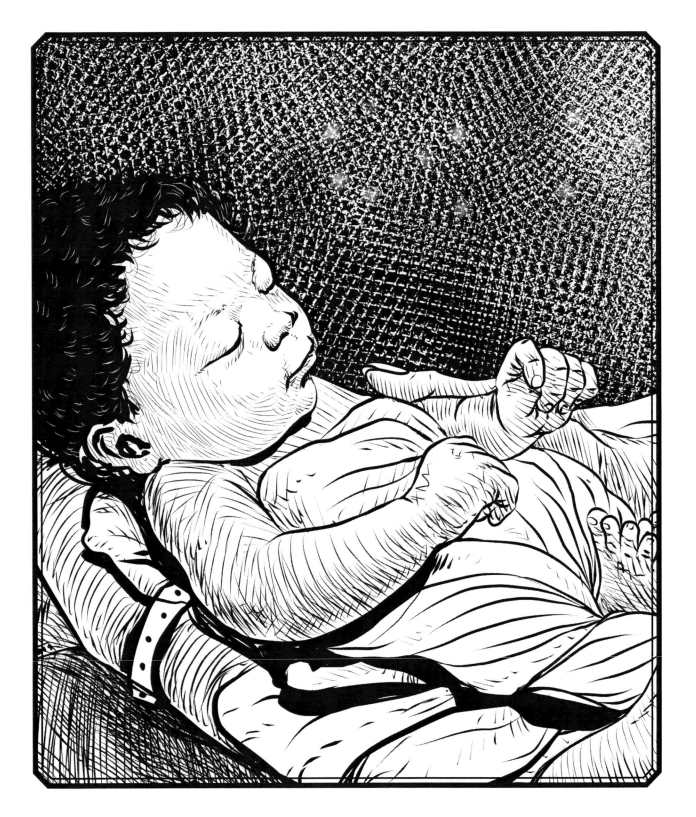

Daddy gives the baby back to Mommy.

She's a little weak but can manage.

She waited 9 months
to meet him,
so she will surely take
advantage.

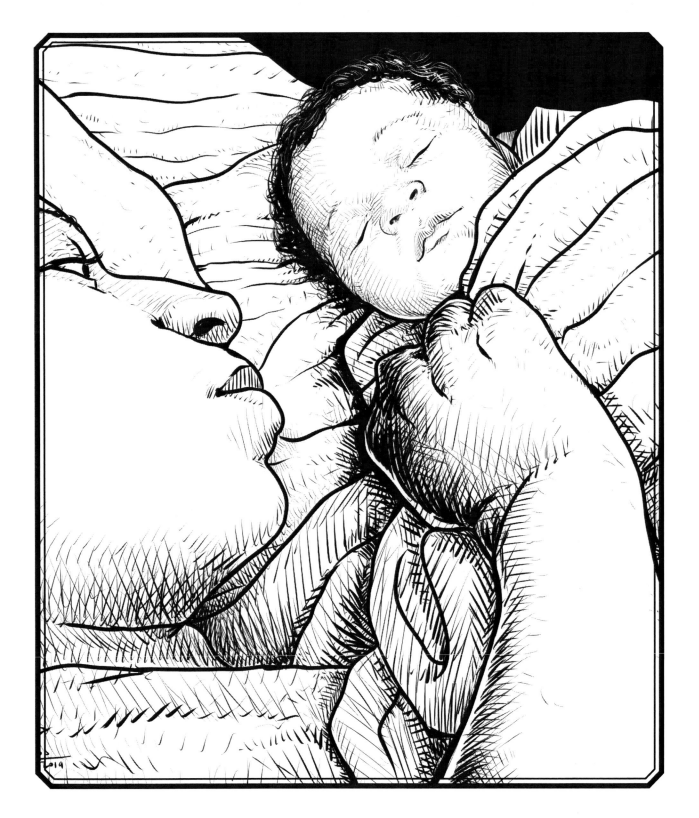

She looks down at Louie.
He looks up at her.

Mommy's heart is full of joy,
holding her little boy.

"How can you love someone this much?", she thinks to herself.

It's unbelievable how you can love another human more than yourself.

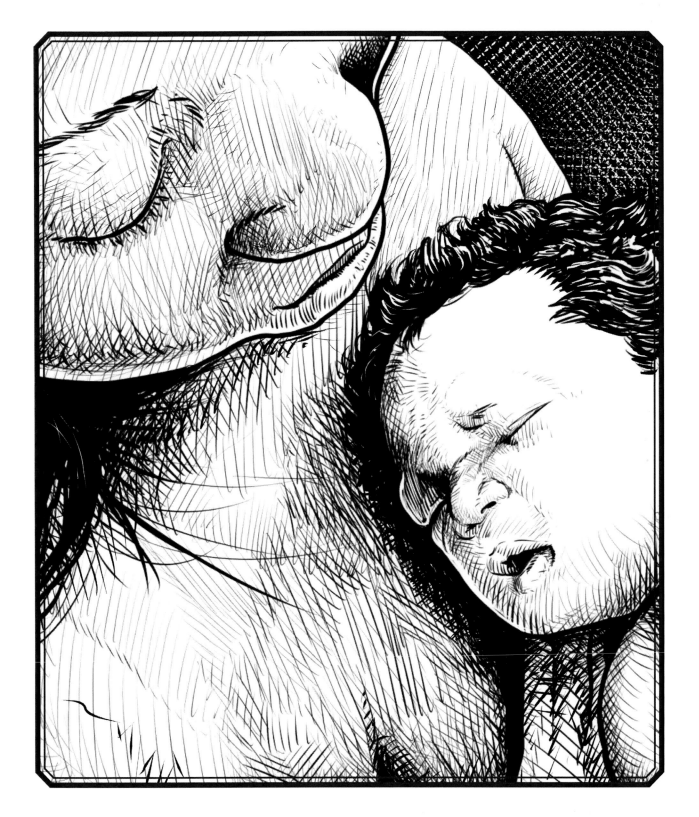

"It's time to get some rest," says the nurse, as she takes Little Louie from Mommy.

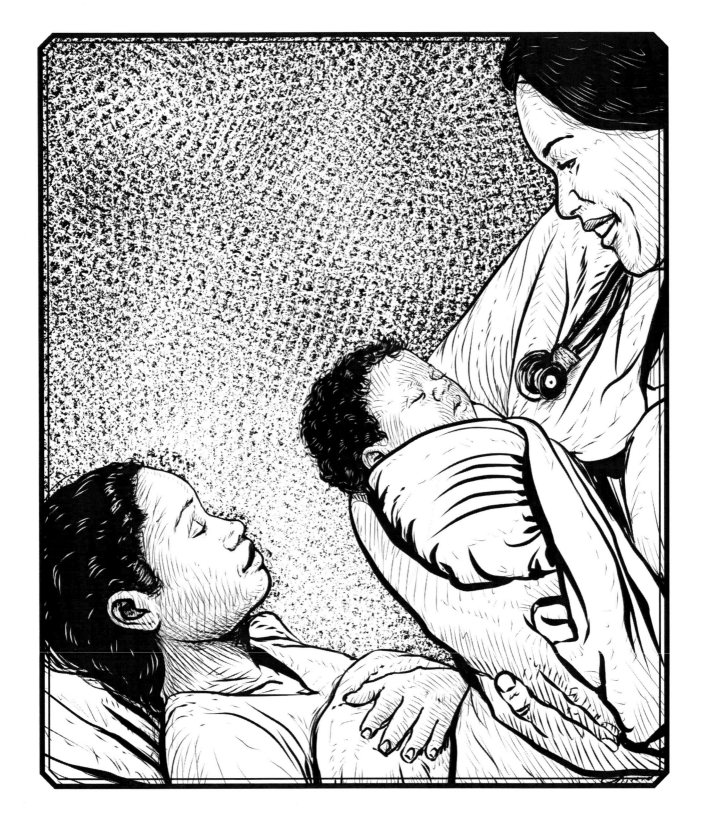

It's been quite a long day
for the brand-new family.

A few days go by and everything checks out well.

It's time to take Little Louie home, where there will be more stories to tell.

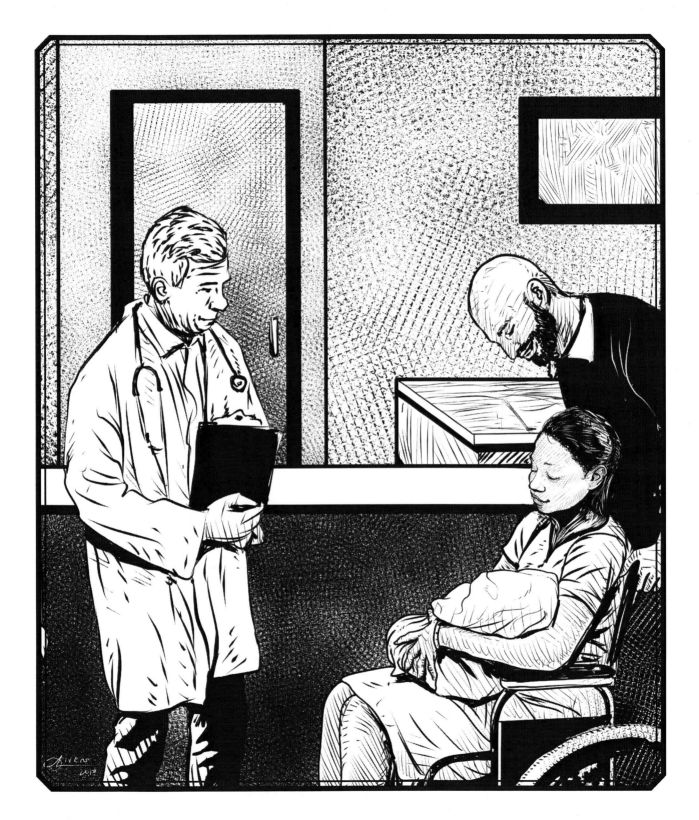

I've shared a bit of my story. Now it's time for you to journal yours. The next section of this book is all about you. Have fun with it. Be real, write down exactly how you feel. Add pictures and fun stats of your labor, delivery and hospital stay. Days, months or even years from now you'll be able to look back and reflect on your very special day!

Journal

- When did you find out you were pregnant?

  _____

  _____

  _____

- What was your initial reaction?

  _____

  _____

  _____

- Who did you tell first?

  _____

  _____

  _____

- When was the very first OBGYN appointment?

  _____

  _____

  _____

- When was the first time you felt the baby kick?

  _____

  _____

  _____

- Did you find out the sex of the baby?

_____

_____

_____

- What did you crave during your pregnancy?

_____

_____

_____

- Where were you when you felt the first contraction?

_____

_____

_____

- Did your water break? If so, where?

_____

_____

_____

- Who drove you to the hospital?

_____

_____

_____

- Epidural or natural birth?

_____

_____

_____

- Who was the delivery doctor?

  _____

  _____

  _____

- Did you have delivery coaches? If so, who were they?

  _____

  _____

  _____

- How long was the labor and delivery?

  _____

  _____

  _____

- What was the first thing you said or did once you saw your newborn?

  _____

  _____

  _____

- Did you nurse or give the baby formula?

  _____

  _____

  _____

- What was the first meal you had after giving birth?

  _____

  _____

  _____

- Funniest moment

_____

_____

_____

- Worst moment

_____

_____

_____

- First visitor and gift

_____

_____

_____

- Last visitor and gift

_____

_____

_____

- Release date

_____

_____

_____

- Who took you home?

_____

_____

_____

- How was the first night at home with the baby?

_____

_____

_____

Memory Verses:

* Every good and perfect gift is from above, coming down from the Father of the Heavenly

lights, who does not change life shifting shadows. {James 1:17, NIV}

* Children are a heritage from the Lord, offspring a reward from him. {Psalms 127:3, NIV}

- Notes

- Notes

- Notes

- Notes

Welcome to the World

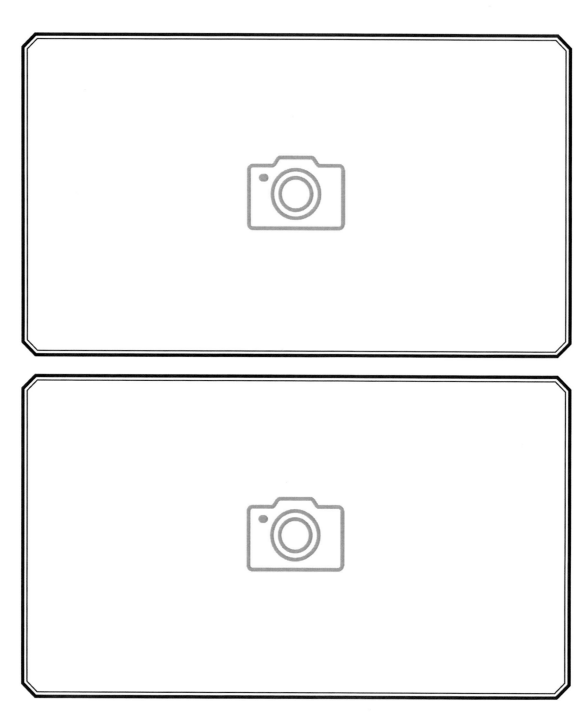

My Baby _____

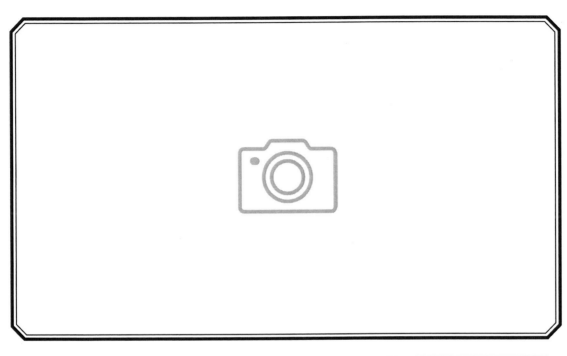

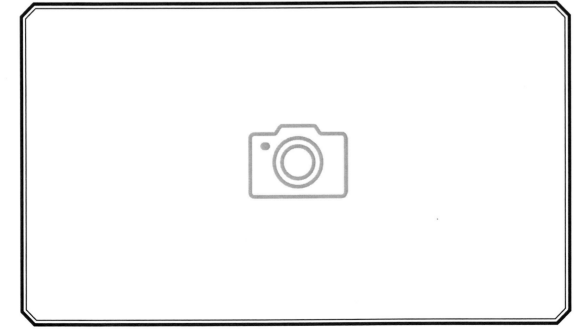

Author's Note:

It's amazing how you feel when you know you're going to have a baby. Personally, I never saw myself having a child. The day I found out I was pregnant all of that changed. I couldn't wait to meet and hold him. Now I ask myself *"what would I do without him?"* I love Louie more than words could ever express. He's my precious gift from our Lord and Savior. One that I will cherish forever.